# The Emperor and the Nightingale

Long ago, there was an emperor who loved beautiful things.
He lived in a splendid palace filled with treasures. Around the palace was a beautiful garden, where he sometimes walked.

But the emperor had never been beyond his garden. He had never been into the forest, where there lived a nightingale.

One day, a traveler came to the palace.
He had walked through the forest
on his way, and he told the emperor
that he had heard a nightingale singing.

"I have never heard a more
beautiful song!" said the traveler.

The emperor sent for his servants.
"Why have you not told me
about this remarkable bird?" he said.
"Bring it to me at once!"

So the servants dropped whatever
they were doing and went off
to search for the nightingale.

They searched everywhere for
a beautiful bird, but found nothing.
Then, when they were about to give up,
they met the daughter of a woodcutter.

"I have heard the nightingale sing
many times," said the little girl.

Then she looked up into the trees
and pointed to a small brown bird
perched high in the branches.

"There it is! That is the bird
that sings so beautifully," she said.

"But it looks so plain and dull!" cried the servants. "It could not possibly have a beautiful song!"

The girl smiled and called to the bird, "Nightingale, Nightingale, please sing."

And the nightingale began to sing, filling the forest with beautiful music.

"Nightingale, your emperor wishes to hear you. Come with us to the palace," said one of the servants.

"This forest is my home," thought the nightingale. "But I will go to the palace to please the emperor."

9

The emperor was surprised
when he saw the small brown bird.
He wondered if it really had the
beautiful song he had heard about.
"Sing, Nightingale," he said.
"Please sing for your emperor."

The nightingale perched on the
back of the throne and began to sing.
Tears of joy rolled down the emperor's
face. Never before had he heard
such a beautiful sound!

"My song has pleased the emperor,"
thought the nightingale. "That is
a rich reward."

11

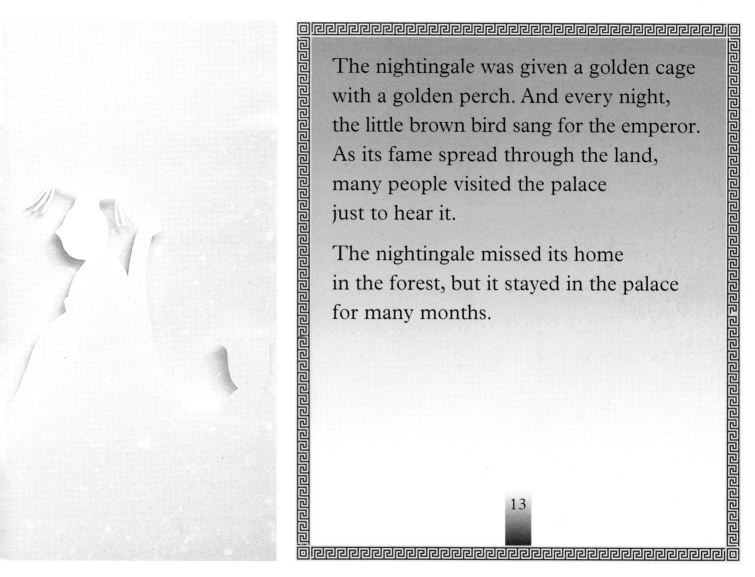

The nightingale was given a golden cage with a golden perch. And every night, the little brown bird sang for the emperor. As its fame spread through the land, many people visited the palace just to hear it.

The nightingale missed its home in the forest, but it stayed in the palace for many months.

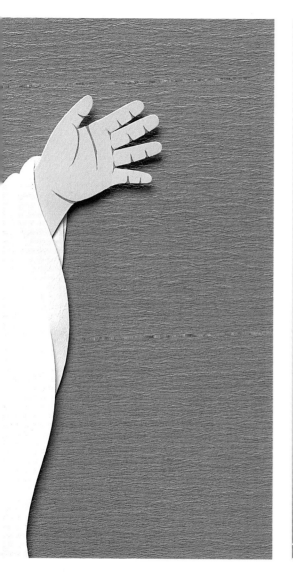

Then, one day, a package was delivered to the palace. When the emperor opened it, he found a toy nightingale, covered in precious jewels. The emperor wound up the toy bird, and a lovely song poured out of the golden beak.

The emperor was delighted with the new nightingale. It was beautiful to look at, and it never grew tired. The emperor listened to the toy bird day and night.

When at last the emperor remembered the real nightingale, he went to its cage. But the bird had gone. It had flown back to the forest, sad that the emperor no longer wanted to listen to its song.

No one seemed to care that the real nightingale had gone.

"This toy bird is truly beautiful," said the emperor. "That other one could sing, but it looked dull and plain."

So the toy bird was given the golden cage that had been made for the little brown nightingale.

17

The toy bird made the emperor
very happy. For a year and a day
it sang and sang and sang.

But one night there was a loud *PING*
inside the toy bird, and the singing
suddenly stopped.

Toymakers came from all over
the land to try to repair the bird,
but nothing could make it sing again.

The emperor was so unhappy that he became ill. Each day, he became more and more unhappy, and each day he grew thinner and weaker. His doctors thought he would die.

One evening, he asked his servant to bring the toy nightingale to his bedside so that he could look at it.

"Please, please sing for me and make me well again," said the emperor – but the golden beak remained closed.

The doctors were in despair.

It was then that the woodcutter's daughter was brought to the emperor. The little brown nightingale was perched upon her shoulder.

"Nightingale, please, please sing for me and make me well again," said the emperor.

And the plain little beak opened, and out poured the beautiful song of the real bird. On and on it sang, filling the palace with its sweet sound. The emperor felt his strength returning.

23

He had tears in his eyes as he listened to the beautiful song.

"How foolish I was to value a toy more than a real bird!" he said.

From that day on, the little brown bird often came to the palace to sing for the emperor. And they were both contented for the rest of their lives.